Rune Divination

By Michael William Denney
www.ThunderWizard.com

Introduction

As I have progressed in my professional Rune
work, I have increasingly wanted to share my
conclusions about specific Rune interpretations that
I have developed in my experience as a
professional Rune reader.

It has been my desire to share some of my
observations with other Rune diviners, especially
those who are new to this field of study.

In my opinion, there are a large number of
misconceptions at large in regard to Runestave
readings based on an inaccurate understanding of
traditional Germanic spirituality and on inaccurate
understandings of proto-Germanic language in
general.

A few of my Runestave interpretations are very
different from many of the more common Rune
definitions out there and I am writing this book to
share some important conclusions I have made in
my own practice regarding Rune divination
interpretations.

As is the case with many of the fields I have studied, initially, I never had any intention of becoming a professional Rune reader.

In the wake of my sudden and unexpected divorce, I was forced to find additional forms of income in order to pay off my sudden debts.

Even though I am a practicing shaman (wizard), I have never considered myself a psychic. My personal experience with most psychics has been less than extraordinary.

In my experience, most psychics that appeared to be accurate were actually very skilled at intuiting my subconscious fantasies. Whether or not this was a result of their cold-reading abilities or whether or not they were able to psychically tune into my subconscious, I am not sure.

But, what I did know was that their predictions, while accurate in terms of my fantasies, rarely came true in real life. So, I wrote off all psychics a long time ago.

Twenty years later, during my research of traditional pre-Christian Teutonic spirituality, I found that my personal Rune readings were proven in time to be surprisingly accurate.

In my early Rune divinations, my readings were focused solely on my personal spiritual path and for friends and students.

Later, when I found myself desperate for income I started working as a professional telephone psychic.

(Insert record-scratch sound effect here)

You might be asking..."*How did someone who does not consider themselves a psychic and who had written off all psychics years earlier get in the phone psychic business?*" ... Good question.

The short story is - I got divorced...

Suddenly, my financial situation was looking grim.

So, I began racking my brain trying to find a way to make some extra money doing things I already enjoyed doing.

One day while under the influence of the Nauthiz Rune, I remembered that I already had extensive knowledge and experience with Rune readings. So, I thought, "Why not see if I could become a professional Rune 'psychic?' "

I knew nothing about being a psychic and it seemed like a long shot, but I was desperate. What did I have to lose by investigating?

To my surprise, within a few weeks, I was working for three different psychic phone lines. I was quite nervous at first. I was not a psychic as far as I knew. Being a 'psychic' seemed a lot different than using Rune readings for personal meditation.

I figured I would simply interpret the Runes as I had always done. If it didn't work, then I would assume that the ancestors did not want me using the Runes in this fashion, I would walk away and look for something else.

My technique was simple. When the phone rang, I listened to the client's question and I would simply lay out the Runes as I had always done for myself and interpreted the Runes I was looking at.

This method worked equally well whether the client gave me lots of information or if they gave me no information. As long as I interpreted the Runes in front of me without projecting my own bias on the reading, the results were almost always very accurate (according to the client, anyways).

Often times, the response was *"Oh my god, that is totally true. You are the best psychic I have ever talked to."*

Well, I wasn't feeling very psychic during most readings. I just simply cast the Runes and interpreted them. I did not know if I was accessing some etheric knowledge or if it was just coincidence or if the client was projecting their own beliefs onto my reading. I didn't really care.

To my surprise, often times during a reading, intuitions and even visions would come to me about the client. Not knowing how true these intuitions were, I would incorporate them into the reading often with very accurate results (according to the client).

The end result of my 'Rune psychic' experiment was that I was making a little money and people seemed to be benefiting from my readings. And, coincidentally, I was getting some real experience learning how to interpret Runes while under intense pressure and time constraints. This was also helpful to my research of pre-Christian Germanic religions.

A result of this experience was that I was able to test out many of my alternative interpretations that I had developed based on researching the connections between the proto-Germanic language and the Rune syllables.

I was able to confirm many of my interpretations with people who had no idea I was using Runes for my entire predictions. But, I also learned some valuable alternative interpretations that I did not originally see in my research.

This book will be a practical instructional on how to interpret the Runes for psychic readings based on my research and my experience as a professional Rune reader.

A slightly different take on Rune Divination

One goal I have with this book is to debunk many of the outdated and incorrect popular Rune interpretations out there.

We are going to take a look at different interpretations of specific Runes based on the needs of the client.

The same Rune in different contexts can mean different things. I will explore some of the different contexts which can affect the interpretations of specific Runes

I will also share with you a shamanic method on how to use the Runes to change possible future outcomes.

It's one thing to look at the future and make predictions. It's another thing to look at the future and choose to CHANGE it. This is possible and very easy to do. I will show you how to do this using the Runes as a guide.

So, whether you are a professional Rune reader or just an enthusiast of Teutonic religious studies or if you just want to find a way to improve your spiritual practice, it is my hope that this little book can provide you with valuable practical tools in your Rune work and in your life.

Enjoy!

The Purpose of This Book
During my previous research into traditional Teutonic spirituality, I developed my own simple system of Rune divination which I used for myself as well as for friends and students.

I have read many books and googled quite a few pages on common Rune interpretations for divination. But, many of the more common interpretations for many of the Runes just did not feel right to me. So, I went back to the Proto-Germanic and Indo-European language as a source for interpretation.

In my version of Teutonic wizardry, I make a distinction between what I refer to as "Rune shamanism" and "Rune divination."

Rune shamanism is a method of self-empowerment focused on a specific method of meditation, breath and chanting (known as 'galdor') designed for personal evolution and spiritual transformation. This is what I refer to as an 'internal' method specific to my version of Teutonic wizardry.

Another method of working with Runes is what I refer to as an 'external' method. This external method is more commonly known as 'divination.' Divination is by far the more popular method of Rune work.

Rune wizardry is a very powerful method of self-transformation and may not necessarily be the best path for everyone. The internal methods in my experience can be very powerful and the resulting energies and forces that are harnessed in these types of practices can be very frightening to those who may not be prepared for them.

(For those interested in the internal methods of Rune work, I refer you to my previous book "Rune Shamanism").

Runic divination on the other hand, is focused externally and is designed to examine what is objectively occurring one's life as opposed to the internal method which is designed to effect change within the individual.

This is not to say that the Rune divination won't have a powerful effect on the reader, but not to same degree as the internal methods.

This book is focused on the external method of Runic divination.

What Are Runes?

So, before we look into my method of Rune divination, I want to ask you to please throw out whatever you may have learned about the origin of the Runes.

The majority of what you may have learned or read concerning the origins of the Runic alphabet is pure conjecture combined with erroneous unconscious assumptions and a handful of half-truths spouted by Western academics who are simply unconsciously perpetuating Medieval propaganda originated by Christian monks designed to minimize or eradicate the extremely ancient origins of our Pre-Christian European spiritual and cultural heritage.

So, let's examine the accepted academic version of the origin of the Runes: (according to Wikipedia)

"The runes developed centuries after the old Italian alphabets from which they are historically derived...The historical context of the script's origin is the cultural contact between Germanic people, who often served as mercenaries in the Roman army and the Italic peninsula during the Roman imperial period (1st century BC to 5th century AD)...

While this is a very logical explanation of the origins of the Runic alphabet it is, however, pure conjecture. I grant you, it is *logical* and *reasonable* conjecture. But, is pure conjecture nonetheless. There is no definitive historical proof as to the origins of the Runic alphabet.

The other problem with the academic theory is that it contains an unstated, unproven and biased assumption which is this:

"The Germanic tribes were unsophisticated, uneducated primitives who could not have originated their own style of writing, so therefore they must have adopted this technology from a superior civilized culture like the Roman empire."

This unconscious assumption is a holdover from the Roman, Christian missionaries who, in an attempt to wipe out pre-Christian pagan European culture, trivialized or demonized pre-Christian pagan culture.

Runes were viewed with derision by Christians (and subsequently by Christian academics) and as a result, the Runic alphabet has never been taken seriously by modern academia in the study of pre-Christian Germanic language or culture.

So, as a result, the Runes are merely classified as an early Germanic attempt to copy Italian alphabets and nothing more.

Before we begin to truly learn Runic divination, we first have to toss out any biases we have unknowingly ingested that may inhibit our ability to allow the Runes to speak directly to us.

So, let's first look at two of the half-truths within the academic theory of Runic origins.

Half-Truth #1
The Runic shapes are based on previous Mediterranean alphabets.

This is entirely possible. However, this statement cannot be proven to be either true or false. The only objective historical evidence connecting the Runic alphabet to the early Italian alphabet is the similarity in shape of some of the characters. Any other connection, however likely, is merely unproven modern conjecture.

What the academics have done here is to start with the unconscious biased assumption listed in Half Truth #1 and made a logical but *unproven* inference based on that assumption which is:

*Since the Italian alphabets and Runic alphabets are similar in shape, and since Rome is the source of true civilization, then the Runic alphabet **must** therefore have a Roman origin.*

The academics are not necessarily aware that they have made this inference, but it is inherent in their argument whether they realize it or not.

While it is not very likely, it is entirely possible that the Runic alphabet symbols have a completely independent origin.

According to the Roman historian Tacitus, when the Germanic tribes performed divinations, they used symbols (presumably Runes) that were carved onto small wooden staves.

The only historical evidence we have of pre-Roman Germanic divination is in this small passage from Tacitus' "Germania." written in 98 A.D.:

"Augury and divination by lot no people practice more diligently (than the Germanic tribes). *The use of the lots is simple. A little bough is lopped off a fruit-bearing tree, and cut into small pieces; these are distinguished by certain marks,* (Runes?) *and thrown carelessly and at random over a white garment. In public questions the priest of the particular state, in private the father of the family, invokes the gods, and, with his eyes toward heaven, takes up each piece three times, and finds in them a meaning according to the mark previously impressed on them."*

Based on this passage, it seems that after the divination was performed, there was no real effort to preserve the staves for future readings. Therefore, any pre-Roman wooden Runic inscriptions would have decomposed very rapidly leaving no physical evidence of their pre-Roman existence.

It was only after the Christian period (which was heavily influenced by Rome) that we find any Runic inscriptions in Stone.

So, from a logical and evidentiary standpoint, I will concede the possibility that the actual shape of the Runic characters may have been influenced by the early Italian alphabet.

But, while the shapes of the Runic letters themselves may have been influenced by other alphabets, (assuming this to be true,) this possibility does not necessitate the conclusion that the *sounds* that the Runic letters symbolized by the physical letters did not have a pre-existing oral tradition within pre-Christian Germanic culture.

It is more likely, based on the uniqueness of the Runic progression of letters, that the Runes had a long-standing pre-Roman oral tradition based on certain sounds that were later reflected in the Runic written alphabet after this alphabet was adopted by the Germanic tribes after early contact with Mediterranean civilizations.

Half-Truth #2
The Runic alphabet was initially created solely for writing purposes. Any symbolic meanings of Runes

used in subsequent divinatory practices were arbitrarily imposed upon the symbols by magicians and priests.

It does seems logical based on the evidence that the written symbols of the Runic alphabet were created for writing purposes.

But, this likely possibility does not necessitate the conclusion that any spiritual properties associated with the Runic alphabet and their corresponding sounds were arbitrarily projected onto the Runic shapes **after** the physical shapes were adopted.

If we compare the Runic alphabet to other existing alphabets, we find there is no other alphabet in existence that shares the same letter order as the Runic alphabet.

This is very significant. And I find it very interesting that the difference in letter order of the Germanic "Futhark" alphabet as opposed to the letter order of other alphabet systems has never been addressed by academics or even by modern Rune magicians.

If the Runic alphabet was merely a Germanic attempt to copy the early Italian alphabet, then the order of the letters of the Runic alphabet would have also been identical to the Italian alphabets.

The Germanic people were and always have been a very practical people. Germanic culture has never had a problem adopting foreign technology of any kind.

If they found something from another culture to be practical and useful, they would see no need to impose any unnecessary details to it. The old adage, "If it works, don't fix it." is a very Germanic sentiment.

If the Runes were merely a tool for writing, the Germanic people would have adopted it in its original form, just as they eventually did centuries later with the Latin alphabet we use today.

The early Italian alphabet progressed in almost exactly the same letter progression as our modern alphabet does today. (abcdef..)

But, the letter progression of the Runic alphabet is not even remotely similar to the Mediterranean alphabets. In fact, there is no other alphabet in existence, modern or ancient that bears any resemblance in terms of letter progression to the Germanic alphabet. The Runic progression of f u th a r k is utterly unique in the entire world.

So, the one question of the uniqueness of the futhark alphabet needs to be addressed if we truly want to understand the origins and purpose of the pre-Christian Germanic alphabet.

If the practical Germanic tribal people did not simply adopt the the Italian letter progression into their alphabet, then that must indicate that the letter order of the Runes had a very significant purpose. It indicates that the f u th a r k progression was consciously maintained.

Since the Germanic people were a very practical and *also* a very religious people, this indicates that the letter progression must have had a very important cultural and spiritual significance that overrode any practical reasons for adopting the Mediterranean alphabets without alteration.

The fact that the futhark is so unique is compelling evidence that this progression of sounds must have had a profound spiritual function to the pre-Roman Germanic tribes.

This indicates to me that the sounds in the futhark alphabet must have existed as an oral tradition long before the adoption of the written shapes of the Italian symbols.

So, in what form did the Runes exist before they were put into written form?

The obvious answer is:
The sounds of the Runic alphabet were part of a pre-existing, Germanic oral spiritual tradition.

Sacred Sound In Indo-European Religion

The Runic alphabet contains the building blocks of all spoken Germanic languages past and present. The Germanic language family is a branch of the Indo-European language group.

Indo-European (IE) languages consist of almost all languages in Europe, the Mediterranean region (Including Italy and Greece) and isolated parts of Asia and the Middle East.

All cultures that speak an Indo-European based language are descended from the first speakers of the Proto Indo-European language group which has its origins in Paleolithic Africa at least 50,000 years ago.

I realize that this last statement may be radically unfamiliar to many readers who were taught the now, disproven Indo-European conquest theory. I do not wish to take up too much space in this book addressing this issue of the recent scientific conclusions for the origins of the Indo-European languages. For more info on this matter, please google "Paleolithic Continuity Paradigm" and/or refer to my previous books including "Awakening Sleipnir."

Modern Germanic languages consist of English, German, Dutch, Icelandic, Norwegian, Swedish, Afrikaans, Scots and Faroese. All Germanic languages past and present are descended from a hypothetical language we call "proto-Germanic" which diverged from the Indo-European language tree possibly at the beginning of the Ice Ages 40,000 years ago.

If I am correct about the origins of the Runic syllables, then we should examine the role of the spoken word in Indo-European spiritual tradition.

Sadly, there are almost no existing Indo-European spiritual traditions that retain an uninterrupted connection to pre-history.

In fact, every single Indo-European religion that existed was eventually abolished and replaced by some form of modern monotheism such as Christianity or Islam.

The only surviving form of traditional Indo-European religion in the world is found in India. The Hindu religion is the only surviving form of traditional polytheist, animist Indo-European religion which can trace its roots back into pre-history.

The modern Hindu religion is an evolution of the Vedic religion and culture which founded the nation of India at least 7,000 years ago. The Hindu/Vedic tradition has been practiced uninterruptedly since that time to the present.

To better understand how traditional Indo-European religion (including pre-Christian Germanic traditions) viewed the power of spoken words, we can look to this concept of sacred sound as seen in the Vedic religion.

In Vedic religion, the spoken word was believed to have immense power. In fact, the Vedics believed that the entire manifested Cosmos was created and maintained by sacred sound.

The Vedic alphabet is studied feverishly by Indian mystics and yogis in an attempt to uncover the mysteries of existence.

All authentic Vedic mantras are examined letter by letter. By examining the differing combination of letters spoken in each mantra, it is believed one can unlock the secrets of existence.

Each letter of the Vedic alphabet (called 'Aksharas') is believed to have its own unique spiritual properties.

The specific letter combination of every true mantra is like an energetic equation which creates a unique spiritual vibration.

The utterance of the correct combination of sounds results in powerful spiritual releases of energy that have the potential to empower the speaker to such a degree that they may be able to achieve supernatural powers or even enlightenment.

I believe it is imperative that any true student of the Runes understand this traditional Indo-European concept of the power of sacred sound and speech.

Runic Alphabet - Building Blocks of Germanic Languages

The Germanic tribes were inheritors of this traditional Indo-European understanding of the nature of sound and speech as being inherently sacred.

Any cursory investigation into the Runic sounds reveals that the Runic alphabet was the basis for all of the spoken Germanic languages.

The later Runic alphabets ('younger futhark,' English 'futhorc' etc.,) were developed relatively late in history as a result of changes in pronunciation in their respective languages. As such, they were derivations from the original proto-Germanic language that was reflected in the so-called "Elder Futhark."

During the time of the common use of the Elder Futhark, all of the Germanic languages still utilized all of the syllables and consonants as they are found in the original Runic alphabet.

As I have previously stated, the inescapable conclusion of my research for me is that the Runic alphabet was an oral tradition created (or discovered) at a time in history during the formation of the Germanic culture as it differentiated itself from the rest of proto Indo-European culture.

This had to have taken place in Paleolithic times in Europe when the ice ages isolated the Germanic tribes from other Indo-European cultures.

In my opinion, based on my research and personal experience, I believe the Runic Alphabet was an oral tradition discovered and used by pre-historic proto-Germanic tribal hunters as method of spiritual and physical survival deemed necessary in ice age Europe.

Each of the three "eights" of the Elder Futhark represent spiritual principles reflected in the three levels of manifested reality popularly known as "mind-body-spirit." In modern heathenism, these three levels of existence are known as "Odin, Villi and Ve."

(For more info on this subject, please read my previous book "Rune Shamanism.")

Rules for Runic Interpretation

1) The Runes are cosmic, spiritual sound vibrations that exist independently in the fabric of the Cosmos.
2) Each Runic sound/syllable has its own unique, inherent spiritual properties and is not subject to arbitrary interpretation.
3) The meaning of each Rune is reflected in the proto-Germanic language.
4) There are no "negative" runes. All runes have a constructive purpose in the evolution of the human being.

There are, of course, many other "rules" about the Rune syllables, but I chose these rules because I believe these rules address some considerable misunderstandings in popular modern Runology and Rune divination.

OK, so let's look at each rule one at a time.

1) The Runes are cosmic, spiritual sound vibrations that exist independently in the fabric of the Cosmos.

According to traditional Indo-European spiritual beliefs, spoken words are a gift of the gods to humanity. In fact, it is the ability of speech that sets humans apart from animals. The act of speech allows humans to become gods themselves.

If the Runes are the Germanic understanding of the sacredness of the spoken word, then each of the Runic syllables and corresponding meanings must have independent existence in the fabric of the Cosmos.

By studying, chanting and meditating on each syllable, we empower ourselves to evolve on a physical and spiritual level.

This leads us directly to the second rule:

2) *Each Runic sound/syllable has its own unique, inherent spiritual properties and is not subject to arbitrary interpretation.*

My biggest contention with much of modern Runology is based in the assumption that the power and meaning of each Rune was imposed upon it by humans.

Without naming names, there are several well-respected Rune "masters" within modern, re-constructionist neo-heathenism who teach that the meanings behind the Runic symbols and sounds are arbitrary meanings that have been magically projected onto the Runes by unknown ancient Rune magicians.

These modern Runologists go on to teach that any meanings contained in the Runes are the result of repeated mental projections by Rune magicians over the centuries.

According to them, it is very important for Rune magic students learn the "correct" meanings of each syllable as it has been taught by their respective schools.

Otherwise, it is believed that the student may be unknowingly projecting his/her own arbitrary understandings onto the Runes thereby confusing or diminishing their power.

This understanding of the Runes being dependent on the arbitrary mental projection of the magician reflects a fundamental lack of understanding of the traditional Indo-European belief in the inherent power of sacred sound and speech.

And, in my opinion, this mistake in understanding demeans the sacredness of the Runes themselves by demoting them to the selfish projections of a few strong-willed magicians.

If the Runes are dependent on our arbitrary projection, then they are nothing more than a cultural peculiarity and have no magical power in and of themselves.

This brings me to the third rule:

*3) The meaning of each Rune is reflected in the
proto-Germanic language.*

By learning the proto-Germanic and Indo-European
root meaning of each of the Runes, their intended
meaning and purpose becomes clear.

This is a much longer subject which will have to be
addressed in the remainder of this book. It is my
opinion after researching the Runes and comparing
the connections between Indo-European root words
and Germanic words, that the inherent meaning of
the Rune syllables must be found within the
language itself.

Such meanings override any modern
interpretations. (Even in some cases with regard to
some of the inconsistencies of interpretations within
the various medieval "rune poems.")

There is some confusion as to the meaning of
certain Runes even as far back as 1,000 years ago
which indicates to me that the Runes reflect a much
older version of proto-Germanic language directly
connected to the roots of Indo-European religion.

And as has been the case with the modern Hindu
religion, many of the archaic meanings of the Runic
syllables have been lost to modern Germanic
speakers over time.

The next rule doesn't necessarily follow the other three, but I found it to be a very important rule in my work as a Rune reader.

4) There are no "negative" runes. All runes have a constructive purpose in the evolution of the human being.

While many of the Runes have a common interpretation, many do not. If you google the meaning of many Runes, you will get a different meaning on each page result.

Among these many and varied Rune meanings are the so-called "negative" Runes. Among some of the more well known negative Runes are, Hagalaz, Isa and Nauthiz, just to name three.

When these Runes come up in readings, they are almost always interpreted as "Stop" "Danger" or "Obstruction" etc.,...

Based on my research and experience, there is no such thing as a "negative" Rune. For someone to interpret them as such in a reading reflects a common fundamental misunderstanding of the original purpose of the Runes.

I will address each of these so-called "negative" Runes on a case-by-case basis. But, suffice it to say, that I highly recommend that the reader discard any notion of any Runes being negative in any way. They can be challenging at times, perhaps, but never negative.

Reading Interpretations

This is a brief interpretation of each Rune stave for general readings. As a professional telephone Rune reader, the vast majority of reading requests I receive are in regards to romance. The second most common readings are in the areas of money and career. The third most common reading request is for a general reading.

The following interpretations are geared toward the professional rune reader or psychic.

Fehu

MONEY

Fehu means "Cattle" and is cognate with the Latin "Pecus" and the Sanskrit "Pashu" which have the same meaning.

Before the use of coin and paper money, the Indo-European people used cattle as barter. The English word "Fee" comes from the proto-Germanic word Fehu and hearkens back to a time when the Germanic tribes used cows as payment.

According to The Roman Historian Tacitus in 98 A.D., the Germanic tribes did not use coin money and did not even keep any silver or gold. He said that the Germanic tribes prized their animal herds above all other possessions.

Fehu in modern times, refers to physical resources of all kinds. It is a fact, however, that modern folk use money to acquire all of their physical resources. So, nowadays in general readings, Fehu almost always represents money.

Fehu is a pretty straightforward Rune. In this regard, my interpretation of this Rune is similar to the popular understanding of Fehu.

Interpretations

Upright:
Increase in money, Promotion or pay raise in work, success in investments or continuation of

acceptable monetary income, getting hired in a new job.

Reversed:
Lack of Money, Loss of Money, Debt, Possibly a Loss of Job or Cut in Pay, Getting Fired or Quitting a Job.

Uruz

POWER

Uruz is the proto-Germanic pronunciation of the word "Aurochs" which is a species of extinct European Bison which was a hold-over from Ice Age Europe. The Aurochs became extinct in the 17th century.

The Uruz was an extremely powerful and ferocious creature. It stood seven feet tall at the shoulders and had very large horns.

Our modern cattle are descended from wild aurochs' that were domesticated by our pre-historic ancestors.

Uruz was an extremely important Rune sound for our ice age ancestors. Because the Uruz provided food, clothing, bones for tools and sinew for lashing and sewing skins.

But, the Uruz also represented the quality of strength and fearlessness.

For ice age hunter-gatherers, bravery and physical power were the most valuable characteristics. Ice age Europe was no picnic and without brute strength and fearlessness, the tribe would not survive.

I have found that in Rune readings, Uruz has some very particular meanings depending upon the context of the client's question.

Interpretations

Upright:
Good health, Determination, Pride, Arrogance, Leadership, (in jobs - supervisory position)

May also refer to a powerful masculine figure - Sexual Virility (especially for males), Domineering masculine nature

Reversed:
Illness, Insecurity, Low Self-Esteem, Fear,
Hopelessness.

In questions regarding romance:
(upright)
Strong sexual appetite, Physical attraction

(reversed)
Sexual Impotence, Feelings of sexual rejection,
Lack of sexual attraction.

*This Rune has a particular recurrence in readings
regarding men who have experienced rejection in
relationships. Often times when this Rune appears
in the placement of the past (left side) it may
indicate that the male in question has experienced
a devastating rejection in romance which has
resulted in feelings of sexual and romantic
insecurity.*

*If this Rune is reversed and placed in the center
and refers to a male, it can mean the man feels
sexually neglected. It can also mean the man has
unresolved insecurities which can make him
irritable or even abusive.*

Thurisaz

BOUNDARIES

Thurisaz is the Rune of Thunor (Thor) the lightning god who is the protector of humans.

Thunor is constantly fighting against the thurse-giants and trolls whose lack of conscious awareness is constantly threatening the peace and prosperity of human evolution.

In Rune readings, this Rune almost always symbolizes what psychologists refer to as "personal boundaries."

Interpretations

Upright:
Safety, Security, Healthy Personal Interaction.

In the upright position, this Rune often indicates that the individual has been successfully working to improve their personal boundaries with others.

Reversed:
Vulnerability, Co-dependence, Allowing Others to Monopolize Time or Energy, Neediness, Passive-Aggressiveness

In Romance, when reversed, this Rune may also refer to infidelity or multiple sexual partners which may result in the loss of personal and spiritual energy for all involved.

In extreme cases, when reversed, it represents the person in question is being physically, mentally or verbally abused.

Ansuz

COMMUNICATION

Ansuz means "ancestor" and specifically refers to the celestial gods who are the ancestors of all humans.

Humans are the only animals capable of verbal speech as we understand it. It is this capacity of verbal communication that is a direct gift of the gods to human beings.

Old English Rune Poem:

"The mouth is the source of all language,
a pillar of wisdom and a comfort to wise men,
a blessing and a joy to every knight."

Here Ansuz is associated with the mouth through which speech comes. It is through the mouth that magical chants are sung. It is through speech that we are able to transmit very complex abstract ideas to one another.

Speech is a mysterious magic that is the true treasure of human beings. A treasure that links them directly to the gods from whom they are descended.

Interpretations

Upright:
Successful Interpersonal Communication.
Successfully Listening to One's Spirit Guides,
Accurately and Effectively Speaking One's Truth.

In readings concerning relationships, this Rune in the upright position signifies that the client is effectively communicating or that the energy of effective communication is available to the client. This indicates that the client should seize the opportunity and take action to communicate with their partner while this energy is available to them.

Reversed:
Withholding the Truth. Denying One's Truth. False Speech. Refusing to Listen to One's Spirit Guides.

When reversed, may indicate that the client is trying to communicate but for whatever reason is not being "heard" by others or does not feel that others are listening to them and their needs.

Raidho

RIGHT ORDER

The word "Raidho" is the root for the modern English words "Right," "Ride" and "Rite" (as in spiritual ritual).

Raidho is a solar Rune symbolic of the regular path of the Sun in the sky.

When we are following our highest destiny in life, we are like the Sun as it follows it's regular track across the sky.

For us to abandon our highest destiny (Orlog) in life, it is as disastrous to us as it would be to life on Earth if the Sun were to abandon her regular path across the sky every day.

Raidho signifies things following their intended path. It represents spiritual law or "righteousness."

Rituals bring us into "Right" relationships with the gods and with the forces of Nature. Rituals allow us to "Ride" the power of our sacrifices which are designed to bring us in line with our highest destiny.

This power of Raidho brings us to our spiritual destinations in life just as "Riding" on a wagon or in a car brings us to our intended travel destination.

Raidho is a Rune of the Soul following her Orlog (Dharma) in this life.

Interpretations

Upright:
Things are "on track." The client is correctly following their destiny. Regardless of the difficulties, the client will be rewarded for their conduct. "Keep doing what you're doing."

Reversed:
Things are feeling "off track." Client is knowingly or perhaps is unconsciously acting against their highest destiny. Involvement in "unrighteous" behavior.

In extreme cases, this Rune reversed can signify someone who is involved in criminal activity. Often times in readings concerning a potential mate or family member, this Rune reversed indicates that the individual in question is breaking the law and/or is in danger of being arrested.

Kennaz

KNOWLEDGE

Kennaz is signified by a torch which lights the way in darkness. The proto-Germanic word "Kennaz is etymologically connected to many words including:
Knowledge
Can (ability)
Gnosis
Shine

This is a very deep Rune that when used personally can effect very deep and powerful change in a person.

For the purposes of general readings, this Rune primarily refers to knowledge, awareness and understanding of self and others.

Interpretations

Upright:
Awareness. Understanding. Knowledge. Education. Mastery of one's chosen field. Study/Reading.

This Rune may indicate that the client is embarking on a time of increased self awareness. In relationships, this Rune may indicate that the couple will gain deeper, intimate knowledge of each other.

Reversed:
Confusion. Lack of awareness.

In relationships, a reversed Kennaz may indicate that the person in question is confused about the relationship or may not know "where this relationship is going" or whether the relationship is right for them.

Gebo

FAIR EXCHANGE

Gebo simply means "Gift" and refers to an equal or equitable exchange of energy.

In pre-Roman times, hospitality was a sacred tradition among the Germanic tribes. According to Tacitus, the Roman historian:

"No people indulges more profusely in entertainments and hospitality (than the Germanic tribes.) To exclude any human being from their roof is thought impious;...They are greatly charmed with gifts, but they expect no return for what they give, nor feel any obligation for what they receive."

In readings this is often a relationship Rune. This relationship may refer to a friendship, casual dating partner or perhaps a business partner. In each case, it refers to a relationship involving an equal give and take.

In questions about career, it may indicate that the client will be "fairly compensated" for their skills and effort. It may indicate recognition for performance on a particular project or perhaps a bonus.

Interpretations

Upright:
Exchange of Energy. Fair Compensation.
Friendship. Casual Romantic Relationship.

In reference to questions about romance: this Rune represents a relationship based on two people who enjoy being in each others' presence. It may represent a long term or a short term relationship. The main signification is that the couple's relationship is based on friendship. In some cases it represents a short term love affair that does not result in a marriage. It can represent a long relationship that does not involve children or formal marriage vows.

Reversed:
This Rune has no reversal.

Wunjo

JOY

This is a straightforward Rune that in divination simply refers to happiness or joy and physical pleasure. For divination purposes, there is no need to elaborate further.

Interpretations

Upright:
Happiness. Joy. Physical Pleasure

Reversed:
Sadness. Disappointment. Depression.

Hagalaz

CLEANSING

The Hagalaz Rune is the Hailstone which falls from the heavens and sometimes comes crashing down to Earth. This Rune is often misinterpreted as being "negative." There is no such thing as a negative Rune. This Rune is a very auspicious Rune that always results in positive, healing results for the client.

This healing may involve some very needed spiritual cleansing which may be challenging to the individual. But, the result is always constructive in the long run.

Ice from the heavens, whether that be snow or hail (Hagalaz is also symbolic of the snowflake) is symbolic of the perfect energy of heaven which comes down to cleanse and nourish in the imperfect realm of manifested reality.

The snowflake represents the pure, undiluted energy of the gods. When this purity touches our imperfect environment the result is always the same: Cleansing and Healing.

This is the Rune of Mother Hulda. Even in Germany today, when it snows people say, "Mother Hulda is shaking out her bedspread." (Traditionally, bedspreads were filled with down feathers.)

This Rune when drawn means that the gods are seeking to clean out old, limiting beliefs and psychological patterns. As previously stated, this can be very challenging but it, like a bitter medicine, is necessary to healing and health.

If there are any unpleasant experiences in association with this Rune, it means that there is decay, disease, dirt that is in need of cleansing.

If one is in good emotional, spiritual and physical health, the challenges associated with this Rune are minimal. If there is unresolved subconscious resistance to needed evolution, the Hailstone will seek to neutralize these self-sabotaging blockages in short order.

If the client is aware that cleansing is coming, they can choose to experience the cleansing as a healing, restorative force. If they choose to resist the emotional, psychological and spiritual changes inherent in this energy, then this Rune can be very challenging.

The more we surrender to the transformative cleansing of Hagalaz, the more smooth and speedy, the cleansing will be. The more we resist, the longer and more challenging the period of cleansing will be.

In my experience, when someone knows that the challenges they are facing are actually a time of spiritual, emotional and psychological cleansing, this will lessen any "negative" experiences.

Interpretations

Upright:
Cleansing, Healing, Purifying, Elimination of Stagnant Energy, Elimination of Self-Sabotaging Subconscious Patterns.

Reversed:
This Rune has no reversal.

Nauthiz

CONSTRAINT

Nauthiz or Naught comes from the combination of two proto-Germanic words: Na + Wight.
Na = No, Wight = Spirit. Na-Wight = "No Spirit" or "No Energy."

It is important to understand that the negation word "Na" does not mean "emptiness" in the usual understanding. It means the emptiness of the power of pure undifferentiated potential. It is only "nothing" because it has not materialized into any specific form. But, it is not without power.

In fact, Naught is extremely powerful. It is so powerful, in fact, that it has not been limited by any specific form.

Nauthiz is another Rune that has been misinterpreted as being "negative." Not so.

Nauthiz is a Rune that heralds the birth of new creation, new invention. For those clients who are privileged enough to have this Rune appear in their reading, they can expect that new horizons are about to appear for them, seemingly out of nowhere. But they must actively search for the solution.

This Rune has been traditionally called the "Need-Fire" Rune. The symbol is of two sticks being rubbed together to create fire.

The symbolism clearly hearkens back to pre-historic times when the only way to create fire was to rub two sticks together.

So, the question is: Who goes to all the trouble of creating fire in this fashion? Answer: The person who NEEDS heat to live.

In ice age Europe, without fire, people died. So, the constraint of being very cold necessitated the invention/discovery of fire.

This Rune reminds us that Need is something crucial to our survival. Without the sensation of need, our ancestors would not have striven to invent ways to create fire out of nothing and they would have frozen to death.

That is the power of this Rune. It means that the Multiverse is pushing us to think beyond our current limitations to invent new ways to survive.

The old adage "Necessity is the mother of invention." is the heart of this Rune.

Interpretations

Upright:
Feeling of being constrained. Feeling trapped. Feeling frustrated. But always with the promise of new avenues of victory that must be actively sought after.

Reversed:
Feeling Hopeless. Dead End. Going down the wrong path.

When reversed, this Rune signifies that the gods are instructing the client that he/she is pursuing a path that has no resolution. When this Rune comes up reversed, tell the client that whatever has brought them to this path is a dead end that must be abandoned.

Isa

INDIVIDUALITY

Isa is the Rune of empowered individuality. Isa means "ice." Its shape is reminiscent of the icicle.

The ice of this Rune is symbolic of the essence of spirit that has coalesced into material existence resulting in the human individual personality.

An icicle is clear and has the potential to transmit the light of the Sun (Soul).

A well developed, self-sufficient personality has the potential to transmit and magnify the light of the Soul into one's external environment.

When this Rune comes up in a reading it usually indicates that the client is entering a time of independence.

This is another Rune that is often interpreted as being "negative." Sometimes this Rune is incorrectly interpreted as Vanity or Egotism.

However, a strong, healthy self image is essential for survival. Without a healthy sense of self, one cannot be helpful to others. The "negative" traits of ego, vanity, pride etc.. are actually a result of a weakened, insecure self-image, not the strong self image typified by this Rune.

The Isa Rune reflects the power of Spirit as it is reflected through the prism of a strong, healthy, self-reliant individual personality.

In readings of romance, this Rune may indicate a period of celibacy, a period when the gods are encouraging the individual to focus on their own individual personal power.

In questions regarding a possible partner, it indicates that the person in question is more focused on themselves than on a relationship.

Interpretations

Upright:
Healthy Self-Image, Individuality, Personal Power, Self-Sufficiency, Healthy Ego,

Reversed:
There is no reversal of this Rune.

Jera

COOPERATIVE RELATIONSHIP

The Jera Rune is comprised of two Kennaz Runes which interlock to form a "gear." The word Jera means "year." The J in this word is soft and is pronounced like a "Y."

A year is a unit of time that is the result of the seasons working together as a whole. The months and seasons interlock, cooperate and flow through time like the gears of a clock. All four seasons

This Rune is often interpreted as meaning "harvest." A closer look at the harvest reveals that it is the result of the interlocking seasons of the year that allows for the crops to seed, grow and mature.

The harvest cannot take place until after all of the individual parts work together to nourish the crops which become ready for harvest.

The words "year" and "gear" are actually derived from the same proto-Germanic word "Jera." The Old English spelling for "year" was "Gear." They are in actual fact, different pronunciations of the same word. Metal gears derived their name from the fact that gears look like the Jera Rune symbol.

The two interlocking Kennaz Runes signify the interlocking of two or more human intellects that cooperate together to create something in the external world.

The sum of the whole is greater than the parts. Whatever is created is the result of a process, a cooperative process of multiple factors working together for the benefit of the whole.

In the context of work or career, this Rune indicates the cooperation between two or more people working on a project to completion.

In romance, this Rune indicates a committed relationship that likely results in marriage and possibly the "harvest" of a family.

At the very least, in the context of romance, this Rune indicates two people seeking to interlock their individual lives to create something in the external world. This either means children or perhaps a family business.

Unlike the Gebo Rune, Jera always refers to long-term committed relationships.

Interpretations

Upright:
Cooperation, Harvest, Team Effort, Group Project, Productivity, Marriage, Family, Children, Family Business.

Reversed:
There is no reversal of the Jera Rune.

Eihwaz

TRANSFORMATION

Eihwaz is the Yew tree which signifies death and resurrection. The Yew tree emits noxious fumes which, if inhaled, can cause illness or, under the right circumstances, can cause someone to hallucinate and perhaps have shamanic visions.

The limbs of the Yew tree can actually grow into the ground and then resurface as new trees. This phenomenon is seen in the Eihwaz symbol itself which has both ascending and descending lines branching off the main center line.

The Eiwhaz Rune symbol represents the spinal cord in the human body. In the spinal cord, the Kundalini Fire of the Ing Rune travels simultaneously up and down the spinal column and when stimulated strongly, this process results in personal, psychological and spiritual evolution.

This Rune, in readings, indicates that the individual is going through a shamanic initiation of death and resurrection. The Kundalini fire of the Ing Rune is being stimulated and is traveling up and down the spinal column. The person will experience a spiritual transformation whether they want it or not.

Whereas the Hagalaz Rune signifies a spiritual cleansing, the Eihwaz Rune predicts a total metamorphosis on every level. As with the Hagalaz Rune, the extent to which the individual resists the change, the more severe the challenges will be.

When this Rune arises in a reading, it is best to let the client know that they are going to experience an intense personal transformation period. In my experience, if the individual knows the transformation process is coming, the challenges

that arise will be more understandable and
therefore easier to endure.

Once again, this is not a negative Rune in the least.
This is possibly the most auspicious of the Runes.
This is the Rune that can transform a mere mortal
into an immortal god.

Interpretations

Upright:
Transformation on all levels, Shamanic Initiation,
Death and Resurrection

Reversed:
There is no reversal of the Eihwaz Rune.

Perthro

WYRD

Perthro is the "lot cup." The pre-Christian Germanic
tribes were fond of games of chance. They would

place dice into a cup, make bets on the outcome and roll the dice.

According to Tacitus, some Germanic warriors were so addicted to gambling that when they had lost all of their possessions, they would then wager their own persons into a lifetime of servitude.

Because of the Germanic concept of honor, even if the warrior lost the bet, he would willingly give up his most prized possession of personal freedom in order to honor the debt. A true warrior would rather die than break his word, his Troth.

The Perthro Rune is a Rune of Wyrd (Weird). We use this word every day to describe the strange, the unusual or perhaps the supernatural. But in ancient times, Wyrd described the three-fold law of inevitable outcome.

Wyrd is the all pervasive web of conscious Life Force energy that determines the fate of all things. Three Giantesses called "Norns" weave the forces of Time out of three threads consisting of the Past, Present and Future.

It is the patterns locked in the past that creates the present moment. The choices and actions taken in the present moment determine the "debt" which must be fulfilled in the future.

When this Rune arises in a reading, it indicates that there is some karmic pattern that is playing itself out.

In personal or work relationships, Perthro indicates that the individuals in question have been drawn together by the Forces of Wyrd in order to fulfill some unfinished business.

In Romance, this Rune can signify that two people have been drawn together, perhaps seemingly against their better judgement. They most likely have been lovers in past lives and they still have unfinished business in this life.

When we meet someone and suddenly feel that we have "known this person forever," this is the laws of Wyrd at work.

When reversed, this Rune can signify that the karmic debt between people has been paid. When people attempt to stay together after their past debts have been paid, this usually means that they tend to argue over nothing. These arguments do not accomplish anything.

These tensions indicate that it is time for the pair to go their separate ways in order to accomplish other tasks assigned to them by their own Orlog (dharma).

Interpretations

Upright:
Unfinished Karmic Debt,
Personal Tensions that are "Working Themselves
Out" for Good,

In Romance: Two people who have been seemingly
"fated" to be together

Reversed:
Karmic Debt Has Been Repaid,
Destructive Arguments That Accomplish Nothing,
End of Intense Relationship,

In Romance: End Of Relationship - Time To Move
On..

Elhaz

SPIRITUAL EMPOWERMENT

Elhaz means "Elk" and the Elhaz symbol represents the antler of an Elk.

The symbol of this Rune is also representative of the shaman whose arms are outstretched toward heaven while he/she projects spiritual power from the cosmos into the external environment.

Whereas the Eihwaz Rune represents Kundalini power in the spinal column, the Elhaz Rune signifies Kundalini power being projected from the body of the Shaman.

My experience with this Rune has taught me that the power of Elhaz consists of Celestial power and Earthly power flowing simultaneously through the shaman's body. The shaman has become a conduit for the dynamic fusion of Heavenly Power and Earthly Power. This is why this Rune has a strong connection to spiritual protection.

In ice age times, the Elk was an enormous creature whose antlers were ten feet wide. This creature was well equipped for defense against all attack.

The most powerful defense against negativity is a strong energy body. When we engage in spiritual practices that empower our auras, we are well defended against all who would do us harm.

When this Rune comes up in a professional reading, it is referring to spiritual power in a very physical way.

This usually indicates that the individual is being empowered with Life Force Energy. It may indicate that the individual is an energy worker, a natural psychic or is engaged in some kind of activity like Tai Chi, Yoga, Meditation or Magical Ritual.

In Romance, this Rune indicates that the relationship has an empowering effect on the couple which they experience as a feeling of physical well-being when they are in the presence of their lover. Their energy bodies become strengthened as a result of their union.

When this Rune comes up reversed, it means that the individual's energy body is being disrupted in some fashion. The individual has been disconnected from their energy body and therefore, their physical and spiritual connection is in danger.

In many cases, reversal of this Rune refers to abuse of alcohol or drugs.

Recreational chemical use of drugs and alcohol weakens our energy bodies and can result in holes in our auras. This reduces the effectiveness of our energy bodies to protect us against physical, psychological and spiritual attack.

Regular abuse of these mind altering chemicals over time results in psychological, spiritual and mental disease.

In professional readings when a client wants to know the state of mind of their lover and this Rune comes up reversed, the first question I ask is: "Does he/she like to party?" or "Does he/she drink regularly?" The answer is almost always "yes." I ask this first, in order to rule out alcoholism or drug addiction.

If this Rune comes up reversed and there is no abuse of recreational chemicals, then it indicates that the individual is disconnected from their energy body and their spirit guides are instructing the client to begin practicing some kind of Life Force exercises such as Tai Chi, Meditation, Yoga or even just any kind of physical exercise.

It means that physical exercise is a necessary component of their spiritual and physical health.

Interpretations

Upright:
Spiritual Empowerment, Shamanic Ecstasy, Spiritual Protection, Strong Energy Body

In Romance: The lovers in question experience a feeling of well being when together.

Reversed:
Weakened Aura, Vulnerability, Alcoholism, Drug Addiction, The Gods Are Prescribing Energy Work,

In Romance: If Reversed, may represent that the object of affection may have drug or alcohol dependency.

Sawul

SOUL

The name for this Rune "Sawul" is actually an older pronunciation for the modern English word "Soul." This is one of the mysteries of ancient Germanic religion that has become obscured over time.

In the original, pre-Christian Indo-European religions, the Sun in the sky was the external manifestation of the eternal Soul of the Cosmos.

The Sun in the sky to the Germanic tribes was a goddess named "Sunna." Even today in poetic terms we often refer to the Soul as "she."

The inner light within the human being was called the "Sawul" by our Germanic ancestors and it meant that they believed that each of us had a Sun within us at the center of our being. Today we call this inner light our Spirit or our Soul.

When the Sawul Rune comes up in readings, it indicates an increase in spiritual power. The client may experience the world "looking brighter."

This is a Rune of boundless optimism and hope. Whenever we interface with our environment through our eternal Soul, we see the interconnectedness of all life in the Cosmos just as the Sun shines its light on all the planets in our solar system.

In these states when we are under the influence of the Sawul Rune, we are experiencing manifested reality through the eyes of the gods themselves.

Our Sawul, our Spirit is descended from the light of the Celestial Powers. We humans share our essences with the Aesir, the Celestial ancestors who gave their essences as a gift to all humans.

Our Sawul is the essence of the Celestial gods, the shining ones. When we connect to our own internal

Sun, our Soul, we re-connect to our most ancient of ancestors, the beings of Divine light we call the gods.

In general readings, this Rune indicates that the client will have a deeper connection to their Soul. The power of the inner Sun will burn brightly for them.

In readings concerning romance, this may indicate that the client will experience a strong Soul connection to their partner, a feeling of knowing the person from past lives.

Interpretations

Upright:
Spirit, Soul, Spiritual Power, Optimism, Hope, Increased Spiritual or Religious Devotion, Luck, Providence

In Romance: Strong Soul Connection to Partner

Reversed:
There is no reversal of the Sawul Rune

Tiwaz

VICTORY

Tiwaz is one of the first deities the Indo-European tribes ever worshipped. Tiwaz is the Proto-Germanic name of the original Indo-European Sky Father god who lived in the North Star. He guided his namesake people, the Teutons (Children of Tiw) to their highest destiny.

The name Tiwaz is derived from the same Indo-European words as "Divine," "Deity" and "Day." The word Tiw can be most concisely defined as "Celestial Power."

Like all of the original Indo-European gods, Tiwaz was a warrior deity. Around the time of the Roman conquest of Europe, Tiwaz was eventually replaced as the head of the Germanic pantheon by Wodanaz (Odin) the god of shamanic ecstasy.

This change of leadership in the heavens represented the Germanic tribes' move to begin a psychic shift away from a mindset of warfare to one of shamanic awareness. *(Sadly, this shift was interrupted by the Roman conquest of Europe and the subsequent spread of empirical Christianity.)*

As a result, Tiwaz retained the role of the god of warfare, victory and justice. This is the general meaning behind the Tiwaz Rune.

I have discovered a few other specific interpretations of this Rune through my professional work.

One interesting interpretation I discovered is that if this Rune has a strong connection to a following Rune, it means that the gods are suggesting that one "surrender" to what the following Runes represent.

For example, If a reversed Tiwaz Rune is immediately followed by an Eiwhaz Rune, it may mean "Surrender to Spiritual Transformation."

Another interesting manifestation of this Rune in my readings is in response to the dreaded "yes or no" type of questions. If this Rune appears, it is a direct answer to the question, (Upright "yes," Reversed "no").

In questions concerning legal cases, this Rune is an obvious answer since it represents the power of justice.

Interpretations

Upright:
Success, Victory, Justice, Power, Authority, Legal Victory

In Romance: (besides other meanings and in reference to males) Fidelity, Strong Protective Partner

Reversed:
Failure, Surrender, Moral Weakness, Servitude, Legal Defeat

In Romance: If Reversed...Possible Infidelity or Sexual Impotence

Berkana

NEW BEGINNING

Berkana is the Birch Tree, the symbol of Spring, Fertility and Birth. This is also the Rune of the goddess Berchta who is still represented in the Alps during the winter festival of Perchtenlauf.

Berchta was traditionally worshipped at the winter solstice to frighten off the dark spirits of winter and make way for the brightness of spring.

Berchta is cognate with the modern English word "Bright." If you have ever used birch bark as a firestarter, you know how bright birch bark can burn.

Birch twigs were traditionally used to make brooms. They were believed to have magical cleansing power to drive away evil spirits. Witches are represented as riding brooms because the birch twigs from which they are made give the witches the magical power of the goddess Berchta.
In basic readings, Berchta generally signifies, fresh, new beginnings. In romance, it can signal the start of a new relationship.

Interpretations

Upright: New Beginnings, Birth, Cleansing

In Romance: New Relationship, New Direction for Existing Relationship

Reversed: Ending, Stagnation, Darkness

In Romance: If Reversed...Break Up, Divorce

Ehwaz

INTUITION

'Ehwaz' is the proto-Germanic word for "horse." It is cognate with the Latin word 'Equus.'

In tribal Germanic society, horses were believed to be sacred animals who had the ability to transmit messages from the gods.

Anyone who has ridden horses knows that these animals have the ability to intuit where the rider wants to go. This relationship is symbolic of humans who have a cooperative intuitive relationship with the gods.

In general readings, this Rune signifies listening to one's intuition, or a close connection to one's Spirit Guides.

In romance, Ehwaz may signify a close intuitive connection where each person can 'feel' what the other person feels. When couples can finish each others' sentences, they have the power of Ehwaz bringing them together.

Interpretations

Upright: Intuition, Listening to Higher Self, Listening to the Ancestor Spirits

In Romance: Intuitive Connection With Partner

Reversed: Lack of Intuition, Not Listening to One's Higher Self or Spirit Guides

In Romance: If Reversed...Difficulty in "Feeling" One's Partner. Lack of Intuitive Connection in Relationship

Mannaz

DIVINE MIND

Mannaz is the proto-Germanic word for Human. In modern English, the word 'man' signifies an adult male human. But, originally this word applied to both men and women as in our modern word 'mankind.'

Humans were called 'Mann' because this word really means 'Mind' and a true human is a fleshly being illuminated by the light of Divine Mind.

Mannaz refers to this Divine Mind. Humans are the only animals that have the spark of Divine Mind.

The first Human was named "Mannuz" because he was the first humanoid who possessed the Divine Mind of the gods.

It is common nowadays for people to confuse Mind with intellect. There is a difference. Intellect refers to acquired knowledge and Mind is inborn awareness of the Divine. Mind cannot be learned, it is a gift of the gods.

The true purpose of the Mind is to reflect the light of the Soul.

In general readings, this Rune refers to empowerment of the Divine Mind within. When this Rune comes up, it may signify that the client has a powerful higher Mind or that the higher Mind is currently being stimulated.

In questions of romance, this Rune may signify a strong mental/emotional connection with a lover. The symbol itself appears to be two Wunjo Runes mirroring each other.

The client may feel that they "get" the other person and vice versa.

In career questions, this Rune may signify a powerful mental and emotional fulfillment in a particular job.

Interpretations

Upright: Higher Mental Functioning, Opening of Spiritual Centers in Brain, Artistic or Mental Fulfillment

In Romance: Strong Emotional/Mental Connection with One's Lover

Reversed: Blockage to Higher Mind, Spiritual Confusion, Lack of Comprehension

In Romance: If Reversed...Unable to 'get' one's partner, Blockage to Communication with Partner on Mental, Emotional or Spiritual Levels

Laguz

EMOTIONS

Laguz means "lake" and in general readings refers to deep emotional expression. These are the emotions that well up from within our subconscious and unconscious minds.

In dreams, often times water, oceans or floods represent powerful emotions. Laguz represents the kinds of emotions that feel as though they might 'drown' us.

Generally, when this Rune appears in readings, it refers to powerful emotions. When upright, it refers to emotions that are being felt and consciously experienced. They may be very powerful and all consuming emotions, but if allowed to run their course, they will eventually subside.

In romance, this Rune represents strong romantic feelings toward a lover.

If reversed, this Rune can signify that the client is in denial. The emotions are either so unpleasant or so powerful that the individual has either stuffed them down into the unconscious or is attempting to do so. If left untreated, these deep and powerful emotions will eventually surface with a vengeance.

If this Rune appears reversed, it is always a good idea to encourage the client to seek some kind of help whether with a counselor or spiritual advisor in order to work through their feelings and avoid a disastrous 'flood' that may cause devastation to themselves and those around them.

Running away from our feelings never works. We must face our emotions or they will drown us.

Interpretations

Upright: Powerful Emotions, Strong Feelings, Deep Caring,

In Romance: Strong Emotional Bond, Intense Love and Caring

Reversed: Denial, "Stuffing" One's Feelings, Emotional Unconsciousness, Unresolved Unconscious Feelings About to Surface

In Romance: If Reversed...Denial of Feelings Toward Partner, Seeking to Deny One's Feelings About Someone

Ingwaz

INCUBATION

Ingwaz is the ancient Germanic deity of internal, spiritual fire. This word is cognate with other Indo-European words for the sacred flame that carries the scent of the sacrifice to the gods. Other variations of this word are found in the Greek *Egni* the Latin *Ignis* and the Sanskrit *Agni*.

The flame of Ingwaz is internal. In general readings it refers to a period of incubation. Just as bread rises in the oven, the Ingwaz Rune represents a situation that needs to "cook."

When this Rune comes up in readings, I generally advise the client to be patient and allow things to finish "fermenting." Ingwaz can often indicate a situation that is in flux and it is best to allow the situation to process itself. When it is time to take action again, the client will know. Until such time, relax and trust the process.

In matters of romance, Ingwaz may signify a friendship that is in the process of transforming into a love relationship. As with the other cooking metaphors, it is best to allow the partner to "cook." Advise the client to be patient. If you open the oven too soon, the souffle may collapse.

Interpretations

Sacred Spiritual Flame, Internal Kundalini Fire, Process of Incubation, Unseen Transformation

In Romance: A Relationship That Is In The Process of Transforming From a Friendship to a Romance

There is no reversal of the Ingwaz Rune

Dagaz

LUCK

Dagaz simply means "Day" and represents the light of the midday summer sun. In ancient times, before glass windows, the Dagaz Rune would be carved onto wooden shutters.

This Dagaz carving was a way to attract the light of the Sun to one's home, so that when the rays of the Sun shone on their house, the inhabitants could open the shutters and let in the light of the Sun to warm their dwellings and drive away the darkness.

In general readings, this Rune signifies that the individual is basking in the sunlight. There is no more powerful sign of luck and the blessing of the gods than to be in center of the Sun's embrace.

This Rune simply means that the blessings of the Soul (Sawul) of the Cosmos is smiling upon you.

I have chosen to interpret this Rune to mean "Luck" because the power of this Rune is very all encompassing. How does one put into words the meaning of a smile or an embrace? Some things go beyond words. The Dagaz Rune is one such thing. Words fail when trying to describe the brilliant rapture of Dagaz.

Interpretations
Luck, Happiness, Joy, Blessing, Prosperity, Spiritual Bliss...
There is no reversal of the Dagaz Rune

Othala

HOME

Othala means "inheritance" and refers to family lands and properties. In general readings it often refers to physical houses or places of residence.

But besides physical homes, this Rune often refers to the feeling of being *at home*.

A true home is not just a dwelling. It is a place of family and friends.

Othala often times, in general readings, refers to the purchase of a new home. If someone is asking "Should I stay or go?" it may mean "staying close to home."

In terms of career, the upright Othala Rune may mean that one feels secure in their current position.

If reversed, it often signifies a physical move or a loss of a home. But it can also mean a lack of support or a feeling of insecurity or not feeling at home in one's job.

In reference to romance an upright Othala Rune may mean feeling comfortable with one another.

In its complete scope, Othala means being surrounded by the warmth and security of friends, and family. Ideally, our home and our family surround us with the feelings of warmth, unconditional support and nurturing. This is the true meaning of Othala.

Interpretations

Upright: Home, House, Family, Physical and Emotional Security, Purchase of a New House

In Romance: Feeling Secure and Nurtured in the Relationship

Reversed: Change of Residence, Selling a House, Loss of Residence, Feelings of Insecurity

In Romance: If Reversed...Feeling Unsupported

The Basic Rune Layout

There are many layouts used in Rune readings.

The Runes being infinite and holographic in nature, they will lend themselves to an infinite number of possible layouts.

But, in my experience, there is only one basic layout that is needed. My preferred layout tells me everything I need to know. I can choose to elaborate in deeper layouts if I choose, but this layout, in my experience, is all that is necessary to understand what the gods wish to tell the client.

This layout is the tried and true "Three Norns" layout.

In my version of this layout, I have a total of 4 Runes cast. The top Rune is the "Woden Rune" which acts as the overall significator of the reading and then the three "Norn Runes" which represent past, present and future.

This layout is consistent with Germanic mythology which resonates highly with the number 3 as reflected in "Odin, Villi and Ve" as well as the mythology surrounding the Three Norns themselves.

This idea of three and multiples thereof are the backbone of Germanic numerology and esoteric Teutonic spirituality.

While this is my preferred layout. There is no absolute rule. For me, simpler is better. You are free to experiment with whatever layout(s) work best for you.

If you want to experiment with different layouts, you can do a search on the internet, copy Tarot card layouts or find some in other Rune books.

Having said that, for those that are interested, here is how I perform a reading with this simple 3 Norns layout:

Shuffle the deck or shake the box or bag or whatever form of Runes you use.

(Without looking) take out the first Rune and place it at the top. This will be your significator or the "Woden" Rune which will be used as an overall guide to the main lesson of the reading.

Randomly choose another Rune and place it on the left. This is the recent past.

Choose another Rune and place it in the center. This is the present situation.

Choose a last Rune and place it on the right. This is the immediate future.

Sometimes a Rune will literally fly out. This is a strong sign that a particular Rune wants to be in the reading. Sometimes your hand will sense which runes want to be chosen. Listen to your intuition. If you do not sense any specific Runes calling out to you, then just simply lay each one out as you randomly select them.

Interpret the Runes from left to right keeping in mind the overall lesson of the Woden Rune. The client may want to get bogged down in the progression of the three Norn runes, but always try to bring the client back to the main lesson contained in the Woden Rune.

In terms of the layout, it is that simple. Interpreting the Runes and applying them to the specific context of the client's question is another matter which may take some practice.

This, of course, depends on the natural abilities and experience of the Rune reader.

The Question of Time

When it comes to predictions, I prefer to avoid questions with a specific timetable. Quite often as a phone psychic I will get questions like, *"When is Bob going to call me?"* or *"When am I going to meet my soulmate?"*

These kinds of questions reflect a fundamental misunderstanding about the nature of time. I will tell you that any psychic who gives out these kinds of predictions, i.e. exact dates, times etc,... is either deluded about their psychic abilities or perhaps is being deceitful. In my experience, very few people have to ability to predict the future with any degree of reliability.

Many psychics make their career based on their "accuracy percentage." How many psychics have you seen that advertise a "98% accuracy" or some such nonsense?

The reason why there are no psychics with a "100% accuracy rating" is because the best that anyone, including a psychic, can do in regards to predicting the future is to make educated guesses based on the most probable future outcome. Runes are very good for this. This is why I use Runes for divination.

Runes are like a barometer for the current state of Life Force Energy. Asking a question and then casting the Runes is a way to get a real time reading on the state of Life Force Energy as it is being expressed through the laws of Wyrd at that given moment.

The Runes are amazingly accurate when showing the past influences and the state of the present moment, but the future Rune only represents _what will most likely happen_ assuming that there are no significant changes in the stream of Wyrd.

Human choices and actions will change that future outcome. This is why I stress the effects of choice to clients. I much prefer helping them determine which choices will give them the best chance for their desired outcome in any situation rather than trying to take a stab at predicting dates and times.

I can tell you that it is very tempting to tell clients what they want to hear in order to get more business. Many a phone psychic falls prey to this temptation and will happily spout unrealistic future predictions in an attempt to keep a caller on the line for as long as they can.

But, in my opinion, a diviner who is sincerely trying to help people will not give out exact dates or times. Not only because this is very difficult to do, but because it presupposes that the client is a victim of circumstances who has no choice in the matter.

In my case, when I get these kinds of questions, I may respond with, *"Well, why worry about when Bob is going to call? Why not save yourself some time and worry and give him a call yourself?"*

Or, I may say, *"When you have finished preparing yourself emotionally and spiritually, you will meet your soulmate."* To which, the client may respond, *"Well, when is that going to be?"* To which I might respond, *"Well, that depends on what you are doing to improve yourself? Because the more work you do to follow your Orlog* (Personal Destiny) *the faster you will draw your soulmate to you."*

If the client is still on the phone with me after that, then I will say, *"What I can do for you is take a look at possible futures for you based on different approaches to your problem and then we can determine the best course of action for you in order to get what you want in the shortest amount of time. How does that sound to you?"*

As you can imagine, some people do not want to hear these kinds of response questions from a phone psychic. That is because many people (especially those who routinely call psychics to solve their problems) are living their lives like victims. They do not like the idea that what happens in their lives is a direct result of the actions they take. Instead, they would rather just sit around and wait for life to happen to them.

Of course, this kind of passive attitude will result in less than satisfactory life events occurring for them. Life is a participatory sport. We get out of it what we put into it.

To better understand this, we need to once again examine the concept of Wyrd...

Wyrd is the unfolding of Life Force Energy in Time and Space according to the three aspects of Wyrd symbolized by the three Norns, *Urd, Verdandi* and *Skuld.*

Urd
"Origins"
Urd means "Primal Origin" or what we call the Past. Urd cannot be avoided. It is the fundamental Life

Force Energy pattern that MUST be expressed in the Present moment. It cannot be escaped.

Verdandi
"Coming Into Being"
Verdandi is the Present moment that is continuously expressing the fixed patterns of Urd.

There is no such thing as a static moment in time. The present is a constantly shifting stream of Life Force Energy that is always fluid.

Unlike Urd, every instant of Verdandi is being influenced by miniscule variations based on choices and actions we make.

Every choice we make in the Present moment immediately becomes fixed patterns in Urd that must be expressed in the Future.

So, it is impossible to sit back and watch reality unfold. The very choice to attempt to retire from life is itself a choice that will have its own consequences.

Skuld
"Debt"
Skuld is the old Norse pronunciation of the modern English word "Should." We say, "You *should* do this or that." "What *should* I do?" This question asks *"What action can I take which will cancel my Energetic Life Force debt to the cosmos?"*

Many have likened the law of Wyrd as being identical to the Hindu concept of Karma. This is very accurate. However, Karma (which is simply, the law of action - reaction) is only one aspect of Wyrd. Karma is really only limited to an aspect of Skuld.

The point I am trying to make here in regards to divination is that the Future has not happened yet. The best that any psychic can do is make predictions based on the likelihood of potential probable outcomes in the Time stream of Wyrd.

As a shaman, it is my job to help people take charge of their lives and actually change their future if necessary. In fact, just by talking with me, one's possible futures begin to change. Just by talking about changing the future, we have already done so.

As long as we understand that we have choices, we begin to create new possible futures from which we can choose to follow.

Since many who call phone psychics want immediate answers and do not want to pay to hear a lecture on the concept of future probabilities, I may alter my tactics in order to best help them get what they want.

In this light, I may change my approach to the client's question, *"When will Bob call me?"* by saying something like, *"I'm not getting a clear read on that. Do you have Bob's number?"*

If the client does in fact have Bob's number, then I can take a reading on what the likely outcome will be if the client chooses to give Bob a call (which is a much better approach to solving the problem than passively waiting around for Bob to call them.)

When I am asked *"When will I meet my soulmate?"* I may also respond with, *"I'm not getting a clear read on that. What are you doing to make yourself available to meet potential partners?"*

Depending on how the client responds will let me know possible readings I can take for them based on different approaches to finding love in their lives.

For example if 'Mary' calls me and asks this question and I respond by asking her about what actions she is taking, I can then take readings on likely outcomes for her, i.e., What might happen if she goes on internet dating sites?... What might happen if she asks out one of her co-workers?, What happens if she decides to focus on her self for a while instead of dating? etc...

When I take readings on these kinds of possibilities, I have a better opportunity to examine what her guides may be trying to tell her, what is the real issue in her life. Then together, she and I can examine different choices for her that might bring her greater fulfillment.

She may have begun the call thinking that she really wanted Bob to call her, but many times after examining what is really going on under the surface, she may decide that dating Bob is an old, self-sabotaging pattern that she really wants to change.

This is the real reason people call me. Whether they realize it or not, what they want from me is to help them determine what their highest destiny is that will bring them the most fulfillment in their life.

Since the Runes are inexorably intertwined with the concept of Wyrd, the highest path of a Rune diviner is not to try and predict a static future, but to explore the different possible threads of Skuld based on the fluctuations of choice.

The job of a Rune diviner is not to simply sit back and predict the future. Your job as a Rune diviner in terms of future predictions is to look at possible outcomes based on different courses of actions and help the client pick which course of action will help them realize their highest and most fulfilling path of Orlog.

The important point here is that WE CAN CHANGE OUR FUTURE!

Just by talking about changing the future, we have already attracted alternative future possibilities to us. The only thing left for us to explore is what actions are most helpful to our progress.

The most likely future will appear. So, that means we often have to take pro-active actions that may be risky or unusual for our characters.

But, our characters are also shaped by our actions. By repeatedly taking different or challenging actions that are out of character for us, we can change who we are on an energetic level.

After disciplined and continued effort, we can change ourselves into people who attract positive futures for ourselves.

But, if we take no action or take no risks, we can expect to get what we have gotten in the past. If this is desirable, then sit back and relax. If, however, you are unsatisfied with the course of your life so far, then start taking bold action. Start making risky choices.

Not sure how such choices will pan out for you? This is where Runes are very helpful. By consulting Runes, we can get direct help from our ancestors and spirit guides.

For even deeper transformation with Runes, you can look into Rune Galdor. This is a different science that I discuss in another Rune book called "Rune Shamanism."

Context Interpretation

When it comes to interpreting Runes, it is important to take into account the context of the reading as a whole as well as the contextual relationship of the Runestave positions in the layout.

For example,

Let's assume that the following reading is for romance and Mary's question is, "How does Bob feel about me?"

You lay out your Runes thusly:
Odin Rune - Berkana
Urd - Laguz (reversed)
Verdandi - Ingwaz
Skuld - Ehwaz

The Odin Rune (Berkana) signifies the general answer to Mary's question which is that, "Bob feels that his relationship with Mary is entering a new beginning."

The next three Runes show how this new beginning is manifesting for Bob.

Urd - Laguz (reversed) indicates that in the past, Bob was unaware (or in denial) of his feelings for Mary.

Verdandi - Ingwaz indicates that Bob's feelings are in a state of transition. His feelings are "fermenting."

He may not be entirely clear how he feels right this second, but he is probably aware that his feelings are changing.

Skuld - Ehwaz indicates that in the near future, Bob will begin to feel a strong intuitive connection to Mary. This is good for a romantic relationship.

Let's look at another example reading: Frank asks,

"I'm having problems with my marriage, what is going on with my wife Luisa?"

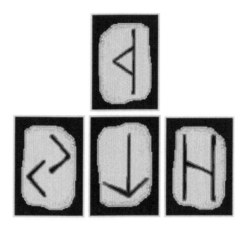

You lay out your Runes thusly:
Odin Rune - Thurisaz (reversed)
Urd - Jera
Verdandi - Tiwaz (reversed)
Skuld - Hagalaz

The Odin Rune - Thurisaz (reversed) signifies the general answer to Frank's question which is that...

Luisa feels that she is either being taken advantage of in the relationship, not getting equal attention in the relationship or that *Luisa may be considering having an affair. "* (This is a sensitive subject, so be tactful when asking the client about either possibility.)

The next three Runes show how this situation will most likely play itself out. (assuming that there are no major actions taken by either party.)

Urd - Jera indicates that in the past, there was a strong marriage bond between Frank and Luisa.

Verdandi - Teiwaz (reversed) indicates that Frank and Luisa in the present moment may need to surrender to... (the Skuld Rune)

Skuld - Hagalaz indicates that in the near future, each of them will have to analyze their past assumptions about their marriage and change their understanding of their roles with each other. This means that they cannot relate to each other in the same ways that they have become used to. They must change as a couple.

The Teiwaz Rune can have other meanings in different contexts. For example, if Teiwaz was in Skuld and Hagalaz was in Verdandi, the contextual relationship between the Runes could significantly change the interpretation:

In this reading, Teiwaz may now mean "defeat" instead of "surrender." Hagalaz in this context may refer to such a thorough cleansing of the relationship that it may be too much for the couple to handle, resulting in a "defeat" of the relationship. (once again, be tactful in such circumstances.)

While I'm on the subject. If challenging readings like this occur, be truthful with the client but also stress that the reading only indicates what _may_ happen if nobody takes any significant action.

If a challenging reading comes up, you can be tacfully truthful, BUT you can also tell the client that if they make some different decisions or take some pro-active action, things could change considerably.

For example, if this reading comes up, you could be honest with the client and tell them that their relationship is seriously challenged right now, but then immediately suggest to them...

"I know this is a challenging reading. So, let me help you out here. Let's take a reading based on what might happen if you and Louisa sought out couple's therapy to address these issues?"

You will be surprised to see how often this completely changes things around.

I could go on and on with more examples, but you will have to learn different contextual meanings of

Runes through your own experience and practice with readings.

The main point here is to learn the basic interpretation of each Rune but also learn how to take into account the contextual relationship each Rune has with the others in the layout.

Further Resources

So, that is a basic introduction into my style of Rune Divination. As I have already stated, I can only give some basic outlines. You will have to learn the nuances of this style of divination through your own practice.

If you are looking to expand your shamanic power base, there are many resources available to you.

If you are strongly drawn to Runes, you may be hearing an ancestral call to the "Old Ways."

For those interested in researching and practicing an authentic path of Mysticism that honors the Old Ways of pre-Christian Europe, here are a few resources I have made available:

www.ThunderWizard.com
This is website dedicated to resurrecting an authentic pre-Christian European path of Shamanism based on Germanic tribal polytheism and Animism.

The Thunder Wizard Path (book)
https://www.createspace.com/3534639

Rune Shamanism (book)
https://www.createspace.com/4059691

Awakening Sleipnir (book)
https://www.createspace.com/3634086

Shamanism for 'White' People (book)
https://www.createspace.com/4040938

Teutonic Shamanism (DVDs)
http://www.dvds.thunderwizard.com

For those interested in very powerful energy practices...

Celestial Qigong Level 1 (DVD)
https://www.createspace.com/306541

Celestial Qigong Level 2 (DVD)
https://www.createspace.com/306925

All of the above resources can also be found by searching for them by name on Amazon.

Keep an eye out for more books and DVDs that are currently in the works...

Thanks for your interest. May the gods of our ancestors bless you on your journey....

Made in the USA
Lexington, KY
19 November 2014